a dog

for all seasons

a dog
for all seasons

JIM DRATFIELD

Clarkson Potter/Publishers
New York

Spring

Springtime is the land
awakening. The March winds
are the morning yawn.

—LEWIS GRIZZARD

If I have seen further [than others], it is because I stood on the shoulders of giants.

—ISAAC NEWTON

Melancholy is the pleasure
of being sad.

—VICTOR HUGO

Friendship is a sheltering tree.

—SAMUEL TAYLOR COLERIDGE

Science has never drummed up quite as effective a tranquilizing agent as a sunny spring day.

—W. EARL HALL

In the spring, at the end of the day, you should smell like dirt.

—MARGARET ATWOOD

April hath put a spirit of
youth in everything.

—WILLIAM SHAKESPEARE

I love spring anywhere, but
if I could choose I would
always greet it in a garden.

—RUTH STOUT

I go to nature to be soothed
and healed, and to have my
senses put in order.

—JOHN BURROUGHS

It's spring fever. . . . You don't
quite know what it is you DO
want, but it just fairly makes
your heart ache, you want it so!

—MARK TWAIN

Those who contemplate
the beauty of the earth find
reserves of strength that
will endure as long as life
lasts. . . . There is something
infinitely healing in the
repeated refrains of nature—
the assurance that dawn
comes after night, and
spring after the winter.

—RACHEL CARSON

The stillness of the early morning scene enables me to take in and enjoy many things which pass me by during the bustle of the day. First, there are the scents, which seem even more generous with their offerings than they are in the evening.

—ROSEMARY VEREY

Summer

Fun is good.

—THEODOR GEISEL

Then followed that beautiful
season . . . Summer . . .
Filled was the air with a
dreamy and magical light;
and the landscape
Lay as if new created in all
the freshness of childhood.

—HENRY WADSWORTH LONGFELLOW

If you saw a heat wave,
would you wave back?

—STEVEN WRIGHT

Ambition is a poor excuse
for not having sense enough
to be lazy.

—CHARLIE McCARTHY

He who attempts to resist the
wave is swept away, but he who
bends before it abides.

—LEVITICUS

I loafe and invite my Soul;
I lean and loafe at my ease,
observing a spear of summer
grass.

—WALT WHITMAN

Summer is the time when one sheds one's tensions with one's clothes, and the right kind of day is jeweled balm for the battered spirit. A few of those days and you can become drunk with the belief that all's right with the world.

—ADA LOUISE HUXTABLE

In summer, the song sings itself.

—WILLIAM CARLOS WILLIAMS

Life is a challenge, meet it!
Life is a dream, realize it!
Life is a game, play it!
Life is Love, enjoy it!

—SRI SATHYA SAI BABA

It was a splendid summer
morning and it seemed as if
nothing could go wrong.

—JOHN CHEEVER

Summertime,
And the livin' is easy.
Fish are jumpin',
And the cotton is high

—DUBOSE HEYWARD AND IRA GERSHWIN,
PORGY AND BESS

The sun is new each day.

—HERACLITUS

The quarrels of lovers are like summer showers that leave the country more verdant and beautiful.

—SUSANNE CURCHOD NECKER

Summer wanes; the
children are grown;
Fun and frolic no more he
knows. . . .

—WILLIAM CULLEN BRYANT

Autumn

Autumn is the bite of a
harvest apple.

—CHRISTINA PETROWSKY

Everyone must take time to sit
and watch the leaves turn.

—ELIZABETH LAWRENCE

No spring nor summer
beauty hath such grace,
As I have seen in
one autumnal face.

—JOHN DONNE

They travel with a constant
companion, autumn.

—JOHANN WOLFGANG VON GOETHE

There is no season when such pleasant and sunny spots may be lighted on, and produce so pleasant an effect on the feelings, as now in October.

—NATHANIEL HAWTHORNE

Listen! the wind is rising,
and the air is wild with leaves,
We have had our summer
evenings,
now for October eves!

—HUMBERT WOLFE

Autumn, the year's last,
loveliest smile.

—WILLIAM CULLEN BRYANT

Be daring, be different, be
impractical, be anything that
will assert integrity of purpose
and imaginative vision against
the play-it-safers, the creatures
of the commonplace, the slaves
of the ordinary.

—CECIL BEATON

And forget not that the earth
delights to feel your bare feet
and the winds long to play with
your hair.

—KAHLIL GIBRAN

All paths lead nowhere, so it is important to choose a path that has heart.

—CARLOS CASTANEDA

We are all in the gutter, but
some of us are looking at
the stars.

—OSCAR WILDE

It was one of those perfect
English autumnal days which
occur more frequently in
memory than in life.

—P. D. JAMES

Winter

The snow itself is lonely or,
if you prefer, self-sufficient.
There is no other time when
the whole world seems
composed of one thing and
one thing only.

—JOSEPH WOOD KRUTCH

Life is too important to be
taken seriously.

—OSCAR WILDE

The ground is hard,
As hard as stone.
The year is old,
The birds are flown.

—JOHN UPDIKE

Winter is nature's way of
saying, "Up yours."

—ROBERT BYRNE

There's a certain Slant of light,
Winter Afternoons—
That oppresses, like the Heft
Of Cathedral Tunes.

—EMILY DICKINSON

Winter is on my head, but
eternal spring is in my heart.

—VICTOR HUGO

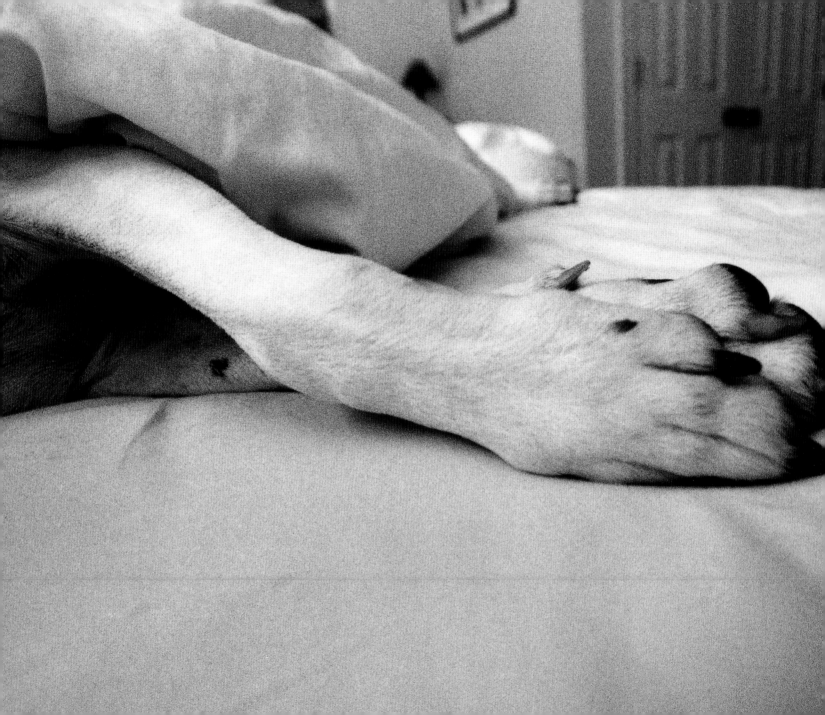

Winter, a lingering season,
is a time to gather golden
moments, embark upon a
sentimental journey, and enjoy
every idle hour.

—JOHN BOSWELL

January is here, with eyes
that keenly glow,
A frost-mailed warrior
striding a shadowy steed
of snow.

—EDGAR FAWCETT

A lot of people like snow. I find it to be an unnecessary freezing of water.

—CARL REINER

We don't stop playing
because we grow old;
we grow old because we
stop playing.

—GEORGE BERNARD SHAW

Acknowledgments

Over the past few years I have had the great pleasure and fortune to be teamed with a crew of top dogs in the publishing world. The following people have shaped my imagery and text and brought it to life with such élan and finesse . . . I thus wag my tail to the following folks:

Lauren Shakely for her continued belief in my artistry.

To Marysarah Quinn, Jane Treuhaft, and Danielle Deschenes, whose aesthetic vision in designing the elements of my books is pure magic.

To Karrie Witkin, who has taken my photography and created alternative and exciting ways to present it. It's always a pleasure to spend time with you. However, as a friend I feel it only proper to warn you: Stay away from selecting the shag carpeting!

To Christopher Pavone, without whose care and faith in my work I never would have had such a blossoming opportunity in publishing.

To my editor, Elissa Altman, in whom I have found a kindred spirit. I am enlivened by the thought of our launching and collaborating on future projects.

To Aimee Kreider, who helped me research the text for this book. I will miss your amazing ability to organize; you have been invaluable in allowing Petography™ to grow.

To the folks at Levine-Greenberg, which is the kind of literary agency that all authors yearn for. I must add a special word of gratitude to my agent, Daniel Greenberg, who has been quite a unique friend, offering candor that not only helps me as an author but has given me perspective on my career. You are a very extraordinary fella.

Finally, to all of you dogs who generously allowed me to explore, via a camera lens, your soulfulness in all of its canine splendor. You continue to teach me how to discover, in an ever maddening world, its wonder.